The United Nations
Leadership and Challenges in a Global World

The History, Structure, and Reach of the United Nations

The United Nations:
Leadership and Challenges in a Global World

The United Nations
Leadership and Challenges in a Global World

The History, Structure, and Reach of the United Nations

Healther Docalavich

SERIES ADVISOR
Bruce Russett

Mason Crest Publishers
Philadelphia

Mason Crest
450 Parkway Drive, Suite D
Broomall, PA 19008
www.masoncrest.com

Printed and bound in the United States of America.

First printing
9 8 7 6 5 4 3 2 1

Series ISBN: 978-1-4222-3427-3
ISBN: 978-1-4222-3435-8
ebook ISBN: 978-1-4222-8549-7

Library of Congress Cataloging-in-Publication Data
on file

Art direction and design by Sherry Williams and Tilman Reitzle, Oxygen Design Group.
Cover photos: Fotolia/Nobilior (top); Dreamstime/Gary718 (bottom).

CONTENTS

KEY ICONS TO LOOK FOR:

 Words to Understand: These words with their easy-to-understand definitions will increase the reader's understanding of the text, while building vocabulary skills.

 Sidebars: This boxed material within the main text allows readers to build knowledge, gain insights, explore possibilities, and broaden their perspectives by weaving together additional information to provide realistic and holistic perspectives.

 Research Projects: Readers are pointed toward areas of further inquiry connected to each chapter. Suggestions are provided for projects that encourage deeper research and analysis.

 Text-Dependent Questions: These questions send the reader back to the text for more careful attention to the evidence presented there.

 Series Glossary of Key Terms: This back-of-the-book glossary contains terminology used throughout the series. Words found here increase the reader's ability to read and comprehend higher-level books and articles in this field.

INTRODUCTION

by Dr. Bruce Russett

THE UNITED NATIONS WAS FOUNDED IN 1945 by the victors of World War II. They hoped the new organization could learn from the mistakes of the League of Nations that followed World War I—and prevent another war.

The United Nations has not been able to bring worldwide peace; that would be an unrealistic hope. But it has contributed in important ways to the world's experience of more than sixty years without a new world war. Despite its flaws, the United Nations has contributed to peace.

Like any big organization, the United Nations is composed of many separate units with different jobs. These units make three different kinds of contributions. The most obvious to students in North America and other democracies are those that can have a direct and immediate impact for peace.

Especially prominent is the Security Council, which is the only UN unit that can authorize the use of military force against countries and can require all UN members to cooperate in isolating an aggressor country's economy. In the Security Council, each of the big powers—Britain, China, France, Russia, and the United States—can veto any proposed action. That's because the founders of United Nations recognized that if the Council tried to take any military action against the strong opposition of a big power it would result in war. As a result, the United Nations was often sidelined during the Cold War era. Since the end of the Cold War in 1990, however, the Council has authorized many military actions, some directed against specific aggressors but most intended as more neutral peacekeeping efforts. Most of its peacekeeping efforts have been to end civil wars rather than wars between countries. Not all have succeeded, but many have. The United Nations Secretary-General also has had an important role in mediating some conflicts.

UN units that promote trade and economic development make a different kind of contribution. Some help to establish free markets for greater prosperity, or like the UN Development Programme, provide economic and technical assistance to reduce poverty in poor countries. Some are especially concerned with environmental problems or health issues. For example, the World Health Organization and UNICEF deserve great credit for eliminating the deadly disease of smallpox from the world. Poor countries especially support the United Nations for this reason. Since many wars, within and between countries, stem from economic deprivation, these efforts make an important indirect contribution to peace.

Still other units make a third contribution: they promote human rights. The High Commission for Refugees, for example, has worked to ease the distress of millions of refugees who have fled their countries to escape from war and political persecution. A special unit of the Secretary-General's office has supervised and assisted free elections in more than ninety countries. It tries to establish stable and democratic governments in newly independent countries or in countries where the people have defeated a dictatorial government. Other units promote the rights of women, children, and religious and ethnic minorities. The General Assembly provides a useful setting for debate on these and other issues.

These three kinds of action—to end violence, to reduce poverty, and to promote social and political justice—all make a contribution to peace. True peace requires all three, working together.

The UN does not always succeed: like individuals, it makes mistakes . . . and it often learns from its mistakes. Despite the United Nations' occasional stumbles, over the years it has grown and moved for-ward. These books will show you how.

The United Nations headquarters in New York City at its fiftieth anniversary.

CHAPTER ONE

Before The United Nations

Since the earliest days of recorded history, rulers of states, kingdoms, and other political bodies have negotiated with each other for the purposes of avoiding or ending military conflict. International agreements and treaties remained valid until they were rendered ineffective by subsequent violations or replaced by newer, more complicated treaties. Alliances were made in this way, through negotiation, sometimes through the exchange of tribute, and even through marriages. War also became an important means of defining relationships between nations, as the victors could then dictate the terms of surrender to the losers. In this way, the earliest forms of international law began to take shape.

WORDS TO UNDERSTAND

amelioration: to make something less severe.

appeasement: a deliberate attempt pacify a potentially troublesome nation.

conventions: formal agreements.

fascist: relating to a system of government characterized by dictatorship, repression of opposition, and extreme nationalism.

nationalism: the strong devotion to nation.

In later times, nations followed a number of **conventions** that governed their interaction with each other. Many of these conventions were informal and could be thought of as guidelines rather than as established law. Over time, more sophisticated systems of government began to evolve. As governments developed and began to rely more heavily on the rule of law, it became necessary to seek a common framework for resolving legal issues between and among states.

Early International Bodies

One of the first international peacekeeping organizations, the Holy Alliance, was a coalition of Russia, Austria, and Prussia (part of present-day Germany) created in 1815. Czar Alexander I of Russia initially proposed the alliance as a means to achieve political action through a common belief in Christianity. It became a tool for absolute monarchs to work together and form alliances against the rising tide of revolution and **nationalism** that was sweeping Europe.

Congress of Vienna, a drawing by French artist Jean-Baptiste Isabey, 1815.

Red Cross volunteers in Bangkok, Thailand, during government protests in 2013.

Another important attempt was the First Geneva Convention. Adopted in 1864 as part of the founding of the International Red Cross, this instrument defined legal and humane treatment for battlefield casualties in wartime. The convention was inspired by the memoirs of a Swiss businessman, Henri Dunant, who witnessed the sufferings of soldiers wounded during a battle in 1859 between French and Austrian armies and who wrote a book calling for the creation of a civilian relief agency to care for the wounded during wartime.

In 1863, the Geneva Society for Public Welfare became aware of the issue and created a committee of five, eventually known as the International Committee of the Red Cross. On August 22, 1864, this committee convened

The Palais Wilson, headquarters of the League of Nations Secretariat from 1920 to 1936 in Geneva, Switzerland. It is now home to the UN High Commissioner for Human Rights (OHCHR).

a meeting of diplomats from sixteen European countries who ultimately created the First Geneva Convention, a treaty designed to save lives, to ease the suffering of wounded and sick soldiers, and to protect civilians who attempted to care for casualties.

The First Geneva Convention, known as the Convention for the **Amelioration** of the Condition of the Wounded in Armies in the Field, 1864, is a good example of how international law is created. Three additions followed the First Geneva Convention, and the treatment of wounded soldiers and prisoners of war has been greatly impacted by the humanitarian activities of the International Red Cross ever since. This was especially true in World War I.

World War I and the League of Nations

As World War I drew to a close in 1918, leaders on both sides were left to ponder the vast destructive power of war on a global scale. The loss of human life, as well as the loss of cities, bridges, and crops, made the total costs of such conflict nearly incalculable. The idea of creating an international body that could prevent future conflicts through negotiation was initially proposed by British foreign secretary Edward Grey, though the Democratic U.S. president Woodrow Wilson and his adviser Colonel Edward M. House ardently supported it as a means of avoiding the catastrophic loss of life seen in World War I.

Evidence of the trench warfare that devastated the countries on the front in World War I still exists, such as this scene in Vacquois, in northeastern France.

The creation of such an organization became a central point of Wilson's proposal to end the war, known as the "Fourteen Points for Peace." The fourteenth point reads as follows: "A general association of nations must be formed under specific covenants for the purpose of affording mutual guarantees of political independence and territorial integrity to great and small states alike." Wilson was a strong advocate of including the formation of the League of Nations in the Treaty of Versailles. On January 25, 1919, the Paris Peace Conference accepted Wilson's proposal to create the League of Nations. A special commission was formed to draft the Covenant of the League of Nations. Ultimately, the League was instituted by Part I of the Treaty of Versailles, which was signed on June 28, 1919. Forty-four different countries, including thirty-one that had taken part in the war on the side of the Triple Entente (France, Great Britain, and Russia), signed the charter. Despite Wilson's devotion to establishing the League of Nations, the United States neither ratified the charter nor joined the League. However, Wilson received international acclaim for his efforts in making the League a reality, and he was awarded the Nobel Peace Prize in 1919.

The first meeting of the League was held in London on January 10, 1920, and its first official act was to ratify the Treaty of Versailles, formally ending World War I. Geneva eventually became the League's headquarters, and the first general assembly of the League was held there on November 15, 1920. Unfortunately, the League of Nations was not a long-term success. The organization met its demise with the outbreak of World War II due to a number of fundamental flaws.

Failures of the League of Nations

Like the United Nations today, the League of Nations lacked an armed force of its own and depended on the armies of member states to enforce its resolutions, which they were very reluctant to do. The most severe measures the League could implement outside of military action were economic sanctions. These were difficult to enforce and had no real effect on the sanctioned country, because it could simply trade with those nations outside the League.

The League's two most powerful members, Great Britain and France, were basically pacifist, or peace-loving, states, following the bloodshed of World War I. As a result, they were extremely reluctant to use military force on behalf of the League. Both governments preferred to negotiate treaties without the involvement of the organization. In the end, Britain and France both discarded the League's philosophy of collective security in favor of **appeasement**, as the threat of German aggression grew with the rise to power of Adolf Hitler.

Another problem the League of Nations faced was the lack of effective representation. Although originally intended to feature representatives from all nations, many influential nations never joined or joined for only a short period of time. The refusal of the United States to join took away much of the League's potential power.

The League was further weakened when the fascist nations began to leave the organization in the 1930s. Japan was originally a permanent member but saw the League as Eurocentric and withdrew in 1932. Italy also began as a permanent member but withdrew in 1937. The League had accepted Germany as a member in 1926, deeming it a "peace-loving country" rehabilitated from its involvement in World War I.

EARLIER DOCUMENTS

On January 1, 1942, with the United States fully enmeshed in World War II, President Franklin Roosevelt, Prime Minister Winston Churchill of Britain, the Soviet Union's Maxim Litvinov, and T.V. Soong of China, signed the Declaration by United Nations, a short document that bound each of the Allied nations together, and prohibited each from making a separate peace with Italy, Germany, Japan, and their Axis allies.

The document also bound each nation to the Atlantic Charter, which Roosevelt and Churchill had earlier signed. The sixth clause of the Atlantic Charter read that the Allied nations hoped "to see established a peace which will afford to all nations the means of dwelling in safety within their own boundaries, and which will afford assurance that all the men in all the lands may live out their lives in freedom from fear and want."

U.S. bombing of an Axis oil refinery in Ploesti, Romania, in May 1944.
The destruction of World War II led Allied nations and the rest of the
international community to establish the United Nations, with a mandate
to ensure future peace, at the end of the war.

However, Adolf Hitler withdrew Germany from membership when he came to power in 1933. The Soviet Union was only a member from 1934 to December 14, 1939, when it was expelled for hostile action against Finland.

The League's neutrality looked a lot like indecision. It required unanimous agreement to enact a resolution, so taking quick and effective action was difficult, if not impossible. This combination of weaknesses left the League ill-equipped to effectively prevent the outbreak of World War II.

The Creation of the United Nations

Following the League's failure to prevent World War II, the nations of the world decided to create the United Nations to fulfill the League's role. At a meeting of the assembly in 1946, the League of Nations dissolved itself, and all of its services, mandates, and property were transferred to the newly formed United Nations. Many agencies initially connected to the League of Nations, for instance the International Labour Organisation, eventually became associated with the United Nations.

The structure of the United Nations was designed to make it more effective than the League. The Allied forces of World War II (Britain, the Soviet Union, France, the United States, and China) became permanent members of the UN Security Council, whose decisions are binding on all members of the United Nations. Like the League of Nations, the United Nations does not have its own armies, but the organization has been more effective than the League in calling for its

The Declaration by the United Nations was signed by the representatives of the Allies in 1942; it was a precursor to the establishment of the United Nations.

members to contribute to missions requiring military force. Examples of such UN missions include the Korean War (1950–1953) and, more recently, a peacekeeping and stabilization program in the Democratic Republic of the Congo, starting in 1999. The United Nations also relies on economic sanctions to enforce its resolutions. Here again, the United Nations has been more successful than the League in attracting members from all corners of the world, giving its sanctions more force. Finally, after decades of negotiation and the hard-won experiences gained through bloody conflict, the international community was able to convene an international body of real significance.

THE UN'S FIRST WAR

The United Nations first flexed its military might during the Korean War, when communist North Korea invaded South Korea. U.S. president Harry Truman urged the UN to take action, and the UN ordered the North Koreans to stop, which they ignored. Truman mobilized the U.S. military and urged the United Nations to send troops, which it did. More than a dozen nations—led by the United States—decided to send troops to help the South Koreans. They would fight under the flag of the U.N.

CHAPTER ONE

TEXT-DEPENDENT QUESTIONS

1. Why did the League of Nations fail?

2. What is the role of the UN Security Council?

3. Which was the first armed conflict in which United Nations became involved?

RESEARCH PROJECTS

1. Use the Internet and the library to create a list of all the "peacekeeping" missions the United Nations has been involved with since its beginning.

2. Research and compare the Covenant of the League of Nations and compare it to the UN Charter. Then create a chart showing the similarities and differences between the two.

British prime minister Winston Churchill, left, and U.S. president Franklin Roosevelt, center, at the Atlantic Charter meeting in 1941.

CHAPTER TWO

Purposes, Principles, and the UN Charter

The UN Charter—the **constitution** of the United Nations—was signed by fifty of the fifty-one original member countries at the United Nations Conference on International Organization in San Francisco on June 26, 1945; although it did not attend the San Francisco conference, Poland did later sign the document and is considered one of the original members. The five founding members (the Republic of China, France, the Soviet Union, the United Kingdom, and the United States) then ratified it, as did a majority of the other **signatories**. It entered into force on October 24, 1945. The United States was the third country to join the new international organization, after Nicaragua and El Salvador.

 WORDS TO UNDERSTAND

amendments: process of changing a legal document.

constitution: an official document outlining the rules of a system or government.

preamble: introduction, or opening words, of a document.

signatories: parties bound by a treaty or contract.

supersede: prevail over; override.

The charter, modeled on the U.S. Constitution, is composed of the **preamble** and a series of chapters made up of the various articles. The document acts as a type of treaty, and all member nations are obligated to abide by the articles it contains. The articles of the charter are also meant to **supersede** all other treaties to which member nations may be party.

The first meeting of the UN General Assembly in 1946.

The UN Charter: Chapter by Chapter

Each chapter of the UN Charter describes a particular area of international law and the obligations of each member nation in regard to that area of the law. The structure and function of the different bodies of the United Nations are also described here.

The first chapter establishes the overall goals of the United Nations as an organization. These include important provisions for the preservation of international peace and security. The text of Article 1 of Chapter I states the following:

> The Purposes of the United Nations are:
> - To maintain international peace and security, and to that end: to take effective collective measures for the prevention and removal of threats to the peace, and for the suppression of acts of aggression or other breaches of the peace, and to bring about by peaceful means, and in conformity with the principles of justice and international law, adjustment or settlement of international disputes or situations which might lead to a breach of the peace;
>
> - To develop friendly relations among nations based on respect for the principle of equal rights and self-determination of peoples, and to take other appropriate measures to strengthen universal peace;
>
> - To achieve international co-operation in solving international problems of an economic, social, cultural, or humanitarian character, and in promoting and encouraging respect for human rights and for fundamental freedoms for all without distinction as to race, sex, language, or religion; and
>
> - To be a centre for harmonizing the actions of nations in the attainment of these common ends.

Thus, Chapter I declares the United Nations to be an international body concerned not only with matters of war and peace but also with all aspects of international cooperation. In addition to describing the purposes of

MANY SUCCESSES

While keeping peace is an important function of the United Nations, the organization has also taken the lead on many issues, including child welfare, the rights of women, alleviation of poverty, and disaster relief, among others.

the body as a whole, Article 2 lists the obligations of member nations, whose conduct must be in accordance with these purposes. It is expected that member nations will be committed to the peaceful resolution of disputes and that the United Nations will use its influence on nonmember nations to persuade them to live in peace.

Chapter II deals with the qualifications for membership in the United Nations. All signatories of the charter are declared to be original members. In addition, Article 4 defines the criteria for nations wishing to apply for membership.

Chapters III through XV make up the majority of the document, describe the various bodies of the United Nations, as well as their respective functions and areas of authority. Some highlights are:

Chapter III establishes the principle bodies of the UN, including a General Assembly, a Security Council, an Economic and Social Council, a Trusteeship Council, an International Court of Justice, and a Secretariat. The chapters that follow provide an in-depth description of the powers of each body. They also establish that men and women should have an equal right to participate in all of these bodies. Chapter VI describes the Security Council's power to investigate and resolve conflicts.

Chapter VII describes the Security Council's power to authorize economic, diplomatic, and military sanctions, as well as the use of military force, to resolve disputes.

Chapters IX and X describe the UN's responsibilities in regard to economic and social cooperation, and the powers of the Economic and Social Council.

Chapters XII and XIII describe the Trusteeship Council, which administered decolonization.

Chapters XIV and XV describe the powers of, respectively, the International Court of Justice and the UN Secretariat.

MEMBERSHIP IN THE UN

Article 4 of Chapter II states that:

Membership in the United Nations is open to all other peace-loving states which accept the obligations contained in the present charter and, in the judgment of the Organization, are able and willing to carry out these obligations.

The charter also requires membership decisions to be made by the General Assembly on the recommendation of the Security Council. Chapter II also outlines provisions for the suspension of member states from the United Nations. The Security Council can vote to revoke the membership privileges of member nations. Nations can also be expelled from the organization. As with membership, this is done by vote of the General Assembly, with the recommendation of the Security Council.

An early United Nations conference in New York City.

The second through the fifth sessions of the General Assembly were held in Flushing Meadows, in the borough of Queens, New York City.

Chapters XVI and XVII outline the procedure for integrating UN policies with established international law. In Chapter XVI, Article 103 states,"In the event of a conflict between the obligations of the Members of the United Nations under the present Charter and their obligations under any other international agreement, their obligations under the present Charter shall prevail." Chapter XVII also reaffirms the treaties made to end World War II.

Chapters XVIII and XIX provide for ratification of the charter and provisions for making amendments.

THE BACKGROUND OF WAR

In the summer of 1941, nearly all of Europe had fallen to the Axis Powers, and bomb-ravaged London, England, was home to nine governments in exile. Although World War II was still in its infancy, all of these Allied nations were looking toward a postwar future. On June 12, Allied representatives met at St. James's Palace and signed a ground-breaking declaration stating that "the willing cooperation of free peoples in a world in which, relieved of the menace of aggression, all may enjoy economic and social security . . . it is [our] intention to work together, and with other free peoples, both in war and peace, to this end."

A Living Document

Even as the charter was being written, all parties were aware that in order for their infant organization to succeed, the charter would need the flexibility to adapt to the needs of its growing membership and an ever-changing world. For this reason, the charter established a procedure to make amendments. Five different amendments have been made to the UN Charter since it first came into force.

An amendment to Article 23 was adopted by the General Assembly on December 17, 1963, and came into force on August 31, 1965. This amendment enlarged the membership of the Security Council from eleven to fifteen. Article 27, Article 61, and Article 109 were also amended at that time.

Eleanor Roosevelt with Pibul Songgram, the prime minister of Thailand, and his wife, at the Roosevelt home in Hyde Park, New York, 1955. Throughout World War II and the years following, Eleanor Roosevelt was intensively involved in international affairs and the establishment of the United Nations.

- Article 27 was amended to require that decisions of the Security Council on all matters would be made by an affirmative vote of nine members instead of seven, including the concurring votes of the five permanent members of the Security Council.

- The amendment to Article 61 enlarged the membership of the Economic and Social Council (ECOSOC) from eighteen to twenty-seven.

- A second amendment to Article 61, which entered into force on September 24, 1973, further increased the membership of ECOSOC from twenty-seven to fifty-four.

- An amendment to Article 109 adopted by the General Assembly on December 20, 1965, came into force on June 12, 1968. The amendment, which relates to the first paragraph of that article, states that a General Conference of Member States may be held at a date and place to be determined by a two-thirds vote of the members of the General Assembly and by a vote of any nine members (formerly seven) of the Security Council. Such a conference would be held for the purpose of reviewing the charter. Originally, the charter provided for a review conference to be held in 1955, during the organization's tenth session.

The charter provides a solid basis for the United Nations to function as an influential body of real international importance. The document not only gives a clear description of the organization's goals, subsidiary bodies, and their functions, but it also is the structure through which the United Nations can adapt to the constantly changing dynamics of global affairs.

CHAPTER TWO

TEXT-DEPENDENT QUESTIONS

1. Which document is the preamble of the UN Charter based on?

2. Which country did not sign the UN Charter in 1945, but is considered one of the original members?

3. Name each of the founding members of the United Nations?

RESEARCH PROJECTS

1. Read the text of Chapter IV of the UN Charter, which discusses the General Assembly, and summarize it article by article.

2. Research the amendment to Article 23 of the UN Charter that expanded membership in the Security Council from eleven to fifteen countries. Write a brief report covering the following: reasons and historical context for the proposal of the amendment, pros and cons expressed by the members and the public at large, and the result of the amendments passage.

The UN's first secretary-general, Trygve Lie, left, and Wallace K. Harrison, the chief architect, seal the UN building's cornerstone in 1949.

CHAPTER THREE

The UN's Policy-Making Bodies

While the United Nations is a vast bureaucracy with many branches, the most basic functions of the United Nations reside in the General Assembly and the Security Council. These two core structures, plus the Economic and Social Council, the Trusteeship Council, and the Secretariat, form the core of the UN's policy-making apparatus.

WORDS TO UNDERSTAND

abstain: not to vote for or against proposal when a vote is held.

budgetary: relating to a budget, that is, a financial plan outlining income and expenses of an organization for a given period of time.

pandemic: a widespread epidemic in which a disease spreads to many countries and regions of the world.

subsidiary: in a supporting role.

validity: acceptance as appropriate and proper.

The General Assembly

The UN General Assembly is one of the six principal organs of the United Nations, and it is its primary policy-making body. It is made up of all UN member states and meets in annual sessions under a president elected from among the representatives. The first session was convened in London on January 10, 1946, and included representatives of fifty-one nations.

The regular session is usually convened on the third Tuesday in September and ends in mid-December of every year. Special sessions can be called by the Security Council, a majority of UN members, or, if the majority agrees, by a single member. Such a special session was held in September 2005 to commemorate the organization's sixtieth anniversary; the session was used to discuss progress on the UN's Millennium Development Goals and to discuss then Secretary General Kofi Annan's "In Larger Freedom" plan. Another special session was held on September 22, 2014, two days before the regular session of the General Assembly, to review the UN's progress on its twenty-year commitment under the International Conference on Population and Development (ICPD), which was approved in 1994 to deliver human rights based on development.

Trygve Lie of Norway was the United Nations' first secretary-general.

Concerns and Voting Structure. Voting in the General Assembly on most issues is determined by a two-thirds majority of those present and voting. Issues requiring a two-thirds majority include recommendations on peace and security; election of members to the UN's principal organs; admission, suspension, and expulsion of members; and **budgetary** matters. Other questions are decided by a simple majority vote. Each member country has one vote.

Except for budgetary matters, General Assembly resolutions are not binding on the members. Assembly resolutions are basically recommendations, or statements of general opinion, rather than binding international law. The General Assembly can address any matters within the boundaries of the UN's Charter, except matters of peace and security under Security Council consideration.

This boy, a refugee of World War II, was one of those who benefited from the United Nations' relief work.

The General Assembly serves as an important forum for members to launch initiatives on international questions of security, economic development, and human rights. This forum is critical because the assembly is the only organ of the United Nations where all member countries are represented, regardless of size, wealth, or influence.

IN CASE OF EMERGENCY

If the Security Council is unable, due to disagreement among the permanent members, to exercise its primary responsibility, the General Assembly may take action on issues regarding peace and security. Adopted in 1950, a series of resolutions known as the "Uniting for Peace" resolutions, empower the General Assembly to meet in an emergency session to recommend action in the case of an act of aggression. Two-thirds of the members must approve any such recommendation.

The Importance of Developing Countries. During the 1980s, the General Assembly became a place to discuss differences between the world's industrialized nations and developing countries. These issues gained importance on the international stage because of the phenomenal growth and changing makeup of UN membership.

In contrast to 1945, when the United Nations had fifty-one members, it now has 193, of which more than two-thirds are developing countries. Having gained strength in numbers, developing countries are now often able to establish the agenda of the General Assembly, define the nature of its debates, and impact its decisions. For many developing countries, the United Nations is the source of much of their international relevance and a principal diplomatic outlet.

The Security Council

The Security Council is the most dominant organ of the United Nations. Maintaining peace and security between nations is its foremost responsibility. While other UN bodies can only make suggestions to member governments, the Security Council has the power to make decisions that member governments are obligated to comply with under the UN Charter.

Decisions of the Council are called Security Council Resolutions. Security Council members must always be represented at UN headquarters so it can meet on a moment's notice to address an emergency

KEEPING PEACE

The first time the UN Security Council approved the use of peacekeepers was in 1948 to keep cease-fires in place in Kashmir, a flashpoint between India and Pakistan, and in Palestine. At the time, the UN Charter did not specifically mention the use of international peacekeepers, but it was codified in 1956 during the Suez Crisis, which pitted Egypt against Israel, France, and Great Britain. UN peacekeepers won the Nobel Peace Prize in 1988 for their work over the decades.

The first meeting of the Security Council in January 1946.

situation; the charter made this requirement to address the inability of the old League of Nations to respond rapidly to a crisis. The presidency of the Security Council is rotated and lasts for one month. The president sets the agenda, presides over meetings, and oversees any crises. The presidency rotates according to the alphabetical order of the members' names in English. The Security Council is comprised of permanent members and temporary members.

Permanent Members. The major Allied countries during World War II—Britain, China, France, Russia, and the United States—are the council's permanent members. In 1971, the People's Republic of China replaced the Republic of China as China's representative to the United Nations. In 1991, Russia became the successor to the seat originally held by the Soviet Union, including the seat in the Security Council. Each permanent member also has the authority to void any resolution, with a single blocking vote no matter how the majority of the members vote.

At present, only the five permanent members are legally permitted to possess nuclear weapons under the Nuclear Non-Proliferation Treaty. Unfortunately, the treaty lacks universal **validity**, as not all nuclear nations are parties to the treaty. India, Pakistan, and, allegedly, Israel all possess nuclear weapons outside the provisions of the treaty. It is also believed that other countries such as North Korea and Iran are working to develop nuclear arms. In fact, North Korea declared it had conducted a nuclear test, which they claimed was successful, in October of 2006, and in 2013 it had conducted a third nuclear test. Thus the ability of the Security Council to prevent nuclear conflict is somewhat diminished as more countries seek, or consider developing, nuclear weaponry.

Temporary Members. Ten temporary Security Council members are elected by the General Assembly for two-year terms starting on January 1, with five replaced each year. These members are chosen by region and confirmed by the General Assembly. The African nations choose three members; the Latin American, Asian, and Western European nations choose two members each; and the Eastern European bloc chooses one member.

In recent years, there has been a movement to increase the number of permanent members on the Security Council. Japan, India, and Germany have all made persuasive arguments for being included as members. Japan and Germany are the second and third largest sources of funding to the United Nations. Meanwhile, India and Germany contribute the most troops to UN peacekeeping missions of all other nations.

One proposed solution is to increase the number of permanent members to eleven. The expanded Security Council would then include Japan, Germany, India, and Brazil as permanent members and include two new permanent members from Africa, most likely South Africa and Egypt. Currently, this proposal has to be accepted by two-thirds of the General Assembly, which translates to 128 votes.

Meeting of the Security
Council in 1995.

The United Nations worked to bring peace in Southeast Asia during the 1970s. Here, a child stands in front of the Killing Fields memorial in Phnom Penh, Cambodia.

Concerns and Voting Structure. The Security Council "may investigate any dispute, or any situation which might lead to international friction or give rise to a dispute" under Chapter VI of the UN Charter. It may also "recommend appropriate procedures or methods of adjustment" if a threat to global peace exists. Such recommendations are not binding on UN members.

When situations arise that pose "threats to the peace, breaches of the peace, or acts of aggression," the Security Council has broader authority. In such situations, it has several options for action, including the use of armed force "to maintain or restore international peace and security" under Chapter VII of the UN Charter. Chapter VII provided the basis for UN military action in 1950 during the Korean War and the use of coalition forces in Iraq and Kuwait in 1991. All actions taken under Chapter VII, such as economic sanctions, are legally binding on UN members.

Most decisions made by the Security Council require an affirmative vote by nine or more members. A negative vote by any permanent member of the council prevents adoption of a resolution, even if it has received nine or more affirmative votes. Countries may also choose to **abstain** from a vote; abstention is not regarded as a veto. Since the Security Council's inception until the middle of 2014, China has used nine vetoes; France, sixteen; Russia/USSR, one hundred eleven; the United Kingdom, twenty-nine; and the United States, seventy-nine. Nations who are not members of the Security Council may be invited to take part in Security Council discussions if their interests may be affected by the outcome of the debate.

"VETO" POWER

The permanent members of the Security Council can, in effect, veto a resolution. A simple "no" vote by anyone of the permanent members is enough to kill a measure. The United States has voted "no" seventy-nine times, although most of those have come in the past forty years as issues concerning the Middle East have come up for debate. The Soviet Union used the veto ninety times, while Russia has used it eleven times.

The Economic and Social Council

The Economic and Social Council (ECOSOC) of the United Nations assists the General Assembly in promoting economic and social development among nations. The ECOSOC has fifty-four members, eighteen of whom are elected each year by the General Assembly to a three-year term. All decisions are made by a majority of the members present and voting, and each member has one vote. The ECOSOC meets annually in July for a four-week session. Beginning in 1998, it has held a second meeting each April with finance ministers who run important committees of the World Bank and the International Monetary Fund.

A separate entity from the many specialized bodies it coordinates, the ECOSOC's functions include gathering information, advising member nations, and making recommendations. It is also well suited to provide

A meeting of the UN's Economic and Social Council in New York in 1982.

consistency in developing policy and coordinating the functions of the UN's **subsidiary** bodies. Historically, the ECOSOC has served principally as a forum for discussion of economic and social issues; it had little real authority. However, beginning in 1992, an effort was made to make the ECOSOC more relevant by strengthening its responsibilities in economic, social, and related fields, particularly in advancing development goals.

These changes made the ECOSOC the oversight and policy-setting body for UN operational development activities and created smaller executive boards for the UN Development Programme (UNDP), UN Population Fund (UNFPA), and UN Children's Fund (UNICEF), which would provide those agencies with operating guidance and facilitate better management. The reform also gave the ECOSOC more power to ensure that UN agencies coordinated their work on issues of common interest, such as narcotics control, human rights, the reduction of poverty, and the prevention of HIV/AIDS.

One positive impact of this reform was the ECOSOC decision in 1994 to authorize the creation of a new joint and cosponsored UN program on HIV/AIDS. This program (UNAIDS) brings together previously established AIDS-related resources and gives them access to the expertise of the World Health Organization, as well as the combined resources of UNICEF, UNDP, UNFPA, UNESCO, and the World Bank. By creating one consolidated global program, the ECOSOC eliminated the duplication of efforts and enhanced the ability of member states to cope with the AIDS **pandemic**. It began operating in January 1996.

FIGHTING AIDS

More than 39 million have died of AIDs around the globe. By 2020, the UN hopes 90 percent of all people with HIV will know whether they have the virus and that 90 percent of all people diagnosed with the infection will be receiving treatment. Of that number, the UN also hopes that the virus will be suppressed in 90 percent of the people infected with it.

A Trusteeship Council meeting at the New York UN headquarters in 1994.

The Trusteeship Council

The UN Trusteeship Council is the last of the principal organs of the United Nations. Its mission was to help ensure that territories under foreign rule were governed in the best interests of the inhabitants and of international peace and security. The trust territories—mostly former colonial holdings—have all now attained self-government or independence, either as separate nations or by joining neighboring countries. The last such nation was Palau, which became a member of the United Nations in December 1994.

Its mission fulfilled, the Trusteeship Council suspended its operation on November 1, 1994, and although under the UN Charter it continues to exist on paper, its future role and even existence remain uncertain. However, formal elimination of the Trusteeship Council would require the revision of the UN Charter, an effort not undertaken as of the end of 2014, despite Secretary-General Annan's suggestion to eliminate the Trusteeship Council as part of his proposed reforms in 2005.

CHAPTER THREE

TEXT-DEPENDENT QUESTIONS

1. How is voting in the General Assembly conducted?

2. How many current members of the General Assembly are there?

3. Explain the role of the Security Council.

RESEARCH PROJECTS

1. Research one of the conflicts in which UN peacekeepers were called to duty and write a short essay about the crisis and the role the United Nations played.

2. Research the various epidemics the United Nations has dealt with in the past twenty years, and create a slide show that includes images and text illustrating one of those outbreaks.

The International Court of Justice meets in The Hague in the Netherlands.

CHAPTER FOUR

The International Court of Justice

The International Court of Justice (ICJ), often called simply "the World Court," is the main judicial organ of the United Nations. Established by the UN Charter, its main responsibilities are to settle conflicts submitted to it by member nations and to give advisory opinions on questions submitted to it by the General Assembly, the Security Council, or by other UN agencies. This court is different from the International Criminal Court, which is often confused with the International Court of Justice.

WORDS TO UNDERSTAND

contentious: characterized by disagreement.

incumbent: necessary as the result of a responsibility.

precedent: established practice; a decision used as the basis of future decisions.

reparation: compensation made by a nation defeated by others in a war.

Structure and Scope of the Court

The ICJ is headquartered in The Hague, the Netherlands. Its fifteen judges are elected by the UN General Assembly and the UN Security Council from a list of persons nominated by national groups. Judges serve for nine years and may be reelected. No two judges may be citizens of the same country. One-third of the ICJ is elected every three years. Each of the five permanent members of the Security Council always has a judge on the ICJ.

Questions before the ICJ are decided by a majority of judges present. The UN Charter states that in arriving at its decisions, the ICJ shall apply international conventions, international custom, and the "general principles of law recognized by civilized nations." It can also refer to academic writing and previous judicial **precedent** to help interpret the law, although the ICJ is not required to abide by its previous decisions. If the parties agree, the ICJ may also rule *ex aequo et bono*, or "in justice and fairness." This means that the ICJ may make a decision based on general ideas of fairness rather than specific law.

The ICJ rules on two different types of cases: states may agree to be bound by the ruling of the court when there is an issue of **contention** between them that they would like to have resolved; the ICJ also

THE INTERNATIONAL CRIMINAL COURT

The World Court, or ICJ, was set up to mediate disputes between governments. It cannot prosecute criminals. However, the International Criminal Court (ICC)—which is not part of the World Court or the United Nations—can bring criminals to justice, usually for crimes against humanity and those involving genocide.

The ICC, also based at The Hague, is an independent body funded by contributions from governments, individuals, corporations, and other organizations. In recent years, the ICC brought several criminals to justice including those responsible for the genocide in Yugoslavia and Rwanda. The ICC is often called into action when nations cannot act on their own to bring a person to justice.

Lake Prespa in Macedonia on its border with Greece. In 2011, the ICJ ruled, in a contentious suit, that Greece violated a 1995 accord when it later objected to Macedonia's admission to the North Atlantic Treaty Organization (NATO).

issues advisory opinions, which provide advice on questions of international law, usually submitted by the UN General Assembly. Several international treaties go so far as to name the ICJ as the authority in disputes over interpretation and application of the agreement.

Contentious Issues

Contentious cases before the ICJ always involve conflicts between nations. The ICJ can only rule in cases where both parties have agreed to bring the matter before the court. If either country fails "to perform the obligations **incumbent** upon it under a judgment rendered by the Court," the Security Council may be called on to "make recommendations or decide upon measures." The Security Council must vote to decide on what action, if any, is warranted.

Unfortunately, the ICJ has historically been weakened by an unwillingness of the losing party to be bound by its ruling, and by the Security Council's unwillingness to enforce consequences. According to the law, however, "so far as the parties to the case are concerned, a judgment of the Court is binding, final and without appeal," and "by signing the Charter, a State Member of the United Nations undertakes to comply with any decision of the International Court of Justice in a case to which it is a party."

The International Court
of Justice building
in The Hague.

The ICJ aims to rule impartially in claims between countries and, in so doing, implements the UN's mission to provide a forum to solve international disputes.

One example is a case called *Nicaragua v. United States*. The United States had previously acknowledged the ICJ's jurisdiction on its creation in 1946 but withdrew its acceptance following a ruling in 1986 that called on the United States to "cease and to refrain" from the "unlawful use of force" against the government of Nicaragua. The ICJ ruled the United States was "in breach of its obligation under customary international law not to use force against another state" and ordered the United States to pay **reparations**. The United States decided not to pay, stating that the ICJ lacked jurisdiction to rule in the case.

Critics often point to the ICJ's unwillingness to take on politically controversial cases. Because the ICJ has no real power to enforce its rulings, its survival is dependent on its political relevance—and that would be endangered if its rulings were constantly ignored by member states. This unwillingness to take on controversial issues is viewed as one of the ICJ's major shortcomings.

Advisory Opinions

The ICJ provides advisory opinions only to specific UN bodies and agencies. When considering a request, the ICJ decides which nations and organizations might provide useful information and gives them an opportunity to present written or oral briefings. The ICJ's advisory procedure is otherwise based on that for contentious proceedings, and the sources of international law are the same. Advisory opinions are considered more as recommendations than as rulings. As a result, they do not generally aim to resolve specific controversies. Certain resolutions or treaties can, however, state in advance that the advisory opinion will be binding on particular agencies or states. Some courts, including federal courts in the United States, are constitutionally forbidden from issuing advisory opinions, but Article 65, paragraph 1 of the Statute of the International Court of Justice expressly authorizes the ICJ to render advisory opinions.

In short, advisory opinions of the court are significant and widely respected interpretations of the law, but they are not enforceable, and they are essentially nonbinding under the Statute of the Court. An example of a past advisory opinion is "The Advisory Opinion of the International Court of Justice of July 8, 1996." This opinion provides one of the few authoritative judicial decisions concerning the legality of the use of nuclear weapons under international law.

In this opinion, the ICJ decided unanimously that any threat of the use of force, or the actual use of force, by means of nuclear weapons that is contrary to Article 2, paragraph 4 of the UN Charter is unlawful. The ICJ also stated that the threat or use of nuclear weapons would generally be against the rules of international law applicable in armed conflict, and would violate the principles and rules governing humanitarian law. Nonetheless, the ICJ's opinion did not conclude, under the existing state of international law at the time, that in an extreme circumstance of self-defense where the very survival of a country would be a stake, the threat or use of nuclear weapons would necessarily be unlawful in all possible cases.

In a unanimous finding, the ICJ further agreed that any threat or use of nuclear weapons would need to meet all requirements of international law relating to armed conflict, chiefly the principles and rules of international humanitarian law, and would also need to comply with specific obligations under treaties and other undertakings that expressly deal with nuclear weapons. In its final declaration, the ICJ decided unanimously that there exists an obligation to actively pursue nuclear disarmament in all its aspects under strict international control.

NICARAGUA v. UNITED STATES

In 1985, the United States was trying to economically and diplomatically isolate Nicaragua's communist government and was providing money and material to the anti-government forces in the country. The Nicaraguan government took the U.S. to court, but the United States walked out of the courtroom on January 18, 1985, charging that the court was being used as a political propaganda tool by the Nicaraguans.

CHAPTER FOUR

TEXT-DEPENDENT QUESTIONS

1. Where is the World Court located?

2. What are some of the limitations to World Court's jurisdiction?

3. What types of cases does the World Court hear?

RESEARCH PROJECTS

1. Research and compare the World Court with the U.S. Supreme Court. Create a chart outlining the differences and similarities between the two. What can you conclude?

2. Create a timeline of the major cases heard before the World Court, including the critical information— the name of the case, the issues important in it, and the outcome.

Secretary-General Dag Hammarskjöld at the UN Plaza in 1953.

CHAPTER FIVE

The Secretariat: The UN's Administrative and Executive Body

The UN Secretariat is a principal organ of the United Nations, headed by the UN secretary-general. An international staff stationed throughout the world assists the secretary-general. The executive arm of the UN system, the Secretariat, carries out tasks as directed by the UN Security Council, the UN General Assembly, the UN Economic and Social Council, and other UN bodies.

 WORDS TO UNDERSTAND

implementation: putting a plan into motion.

mediation: the process of resolving a dispute.

rejuvenate: to restore something to its original condition.

subsequent: later or following.

unanimous: when a group fully agrees.

How the Secretariat Operates

The UN Charter provides that the staff shall not take advice or direction from any authority other than the United Nations. Member nations respect this aspect of the Secretariat and should not seek to influence its members. The secretary-general alone chooses the staff and is responsible for maintaining a pool of talented individuals from all across the globe.

The secretary-general works to resolve international disputes, administers peacekeeping operations, arranges for international conferences, does research for the **implementation** of Security Council decisions, and consults with member governments regarding various programs. Main Secretariat offices in this area include the Office of the Coordinator of Humanitarian Affairs and the Department of Peacekeeping Operations. The secretary-general may draw to the attention of the Security Council any issue that, in his or her opinion, may threaten international peace and security.

As the UN's "chief administrative officer," the secretary-general has an important role to play in international affairs. The position was initially designed to be purely administrative. However, Trygve Lie, the first secretary-general, set a precedent when he chose to magnify his responsibilities and act as a world leader and mediator. Every secretary-general to follow him has spoken out on global issues and worked to maintain peace through **mediation**.

UN SECRETARIES-GENERAL

Trygve Lie (Norway) February 1946–November 1952
Dag Hammarskjöld (Sweden) April 1953–September 1961
U Thant (Burma, now Myanmar) November 1961–December 1971
Kurt Waldheim (Austria) January 1972–December 1981
Javier Pérez de Cuéllar (Peru) January 1982–December 1991
Boutros Boutros-Ghali (Egypt) January 1992–December 1996
Kofi Annan (Ghana) January 1997–December 2006
Ban Ki-moon (South Korea) January 2007– present

Secretary-General Dag Hammarskjold in the Congo in 1960.

Term and Selection of the Secretary-General

The secretary-general is elected to a five-year term. Traditionally, each secretary-general serves two terms in office. By convention, the position of secretary-general rotates by geographic region. An exception to this rule was made with the selection of Kofi Annan. When Boutros Boutros-Ghali of Egypt served only one term, another African, Kofi Annan of Ghana, was chosen to succeed him. When Annan had finished his first term, member states were so impressed with his performance that he was selected for a second term despite the fact that it was now time to select a candidate from Asia. Upon the expiration of Annan's second term, Ban Ki-moon, from one of Asia's fast-growing nations, South Korea, succeeded him and is himself scheduled to be replaced at the beginning of 2017. There has never been a secretary-general from North America.

U Thant of Burma was the United Nations' third secretary-general.

Most secretaries-general come from medium-sized countries or "middle powers" with little prior fame. Although high-profile candidates are frequently mentioned as next in line for the job, these are almost always rejected. Examples of such figures who were rejected for the post include Charles de Gaulle, Dwight Eisenhower, and Anthony Eden, all rejected in favor of the little known Norwegian Trygve Lie.

The Eighth Secretary General

Ban Ki-moon of South Korea is the eighth secretary-general of the United Nations. He took office on January 1, 2007, and on June 21, 2011, he was **unanimously** re-elected by the General Assembly and will continue to serve until December 31, 2016. Highlights of his tenure, taken from his UN Web page, are presented below.

> **Promoting sustainable development**. One of the Secretary-General's first major initiatives was the 2007 Climate Change Summit, followed by extensive diplomatic efforts that have helped put the issue at the forefront of the global agenda. **Subsequent** efforts to focus on the world's main anti-poverty targets, the Millennium Development Goals, have generated more than $60 billion in pledges....

Ban Ki-moon, UN secretary-general
serving from 2007 until 2016.

IN BAN KI-MOON'S WORDS

"I grew up in war", said Ban Ki Moon, UN secretary-general, "and saw the United Nations help my country to recover and rebuild. That experience was a big part of what led me to pursue a career in public service. As Secretary-General, I am determined to see this Organization deliver tangible, meaningful results that advance peace, development and human rights."

Empowering women. The Secretary-General pressed successfully for the creation of UN Women, a major new agency that consolidates the UN's work in this area. . . . Within the UN itself, the Secretary-General has increased the number of women in senior management positions by more than 40 per cent, reaching the highest level in the Organization's history.

Supporting countries facing crisis or instability. The Secretary-General has sought to strengthen UN peace efforts, including through the New Horizons peacekeeping initiative, the Global Field Support Strategy and the Civilian Capacity Review, a package of steps to improve the impact of the 120,000 United Nations "blue helmets" operating in the world's conflict zones. . . . He has also sought to strengthen humanitarian response in the aftermath of mega-disasters in Myanmar (2008), Haiti (2010) and Pakistan (2010), and mobilized UN support for the democratic transitions in North Africa and the Middle East.

Generating new momentum on disarmament, arms control and non-proliferation. The Secretary-General has sought to rejuvenate the disarmament agenda through a five-point plan, efforts to break the deadlock at the Conference on Disarmament and renewed attention to nuclear safety and security in the aftermath of the tragedy at the Fukushima Daiichi Nuclear Power Plant.

Strengthening the UN. The Secretary-General has introduced new measures aimed at making the United Nations more transparent, effective and efficient.

CHAPTER FIVE

TEXT-DEPENDENT QUESTIONS

1. From what region of the world has a secretary-general never been selected?

2. Where do most secretaries-general come from?

3. How many years are in a term for secretary-general?

RESEARCH PROJECTS

1. Research one of the secretaries-general mentioned in the text and write a four-page biography of that person.

2. Research a resolution made by the Security Council. Describe the situation that brought the matter before the Security Council, and what action it took in response. Was the action of the Security Council effective?

All members states are involved in funding the operations of the United Nations.

CHAPTER SIX

Financing the
United Nations

The United Nations budget for the 2012–2013 fiscal year was just over $5 billion for regular operations and over $7 billion for peacekeeping operations. These amounts are small compared to most national budgets, and it is just a tiny fraction of the world's total defense spending. Yet for the past two decades, the United Nations constantly grapples with underfunding and is often forced to eliminate or cut back on important programs in several areas.

WORDS TO UNDERSTAND

arrears: unpaid debts by a debtor that have accumulated.

bond: a type of debt issued to investors who help governments or corporations to finance certain endeavors.

gross domestic product: total value of all goods and services produced within a country.

per capita income: average amount earned by each individual in a country.

prorated: divided proportionately.

Many proposals for UN reform deal with reorganizing its funding system. Some suggest that the United Nations must seek alternative means to fund its programs. Proposed alternatives include establishing a global tax on currency transactions, environmental taxes, and taxes on the arms trade. However, member nations responsible for the highest contributions are hesitant to reform the system for fear they could lose political influence.

The Assessment System

The United Nations funds its programs through a system of assessments by which each member nation is billed for its membership according to a specific formula based on their ability to pay. According to this formula, the United States, which has the world's largest economy, is also the largest

The schooling of children is made possible in part through UN programs.

FORMULA FOR UN DUES

The formula for calculating a country's dues relates to their assessed share of the UN's regular budget and its peacekeeping budgets. Dues are based on their relative ability to pay, calculated from a ten-year average of each country's **gross domestic product**, with reductions made for low **per capita income** and high foreign debt.

contributor to the UN budget, but for some time the U.S. Congress refused to pay its full assessment, reasons for which are described below. In 2009, that changed, but in 2014 the budget approved by Congress for the UN was again below the required amount.

Additionally, many member states have not paid their full dues and have cut their donations to the UN's voluntary funds. Sometimes they refuse to pay a portion of their dues, citing that the money would be used to support this or that program to which they are opposed.

History of UN Funding Issues

The United Nations has faced financial difficulties from its earliest years. Members paid late or fell into arrears. But the first true financial crises arose over early peacekeeping operations.

Peacekeeping Operations. In 1956, the first major peacekeeping operation in the Sinai Peninsula in the Middle East set off a dispute over who should pay, since there was no clear precedent. Several states refused to pay their share, some on the grounds that those responsible for the crisis should bear the cost. In the 1960s, a large and divisive peacekeeping operation in the Congo led a number of countries again to withhold payments because they disagreed with the action. The Congo mission was by far the most expensive ever mounted, so it set off an especially serious financial crisis. The Soviet Union, with its relatively large assessment, led the list of UN debtors.

Without adequate funding, the UN might not be able to conduct relief efforts such as this UN search-and-rescue mission, undertaken and supported by the United Kingdom, after the devastating 2010 earthquake that hit the Caribbean island of Haiti.

The General Assembly resolved the Congo financial crisis by authorizing a UN **bond** issue to cover unpaid assessments. Altogether, the United Nations issued $169 million in bonds in 1960s. The UN later paid off the bonds from regular assessment income. In turn, some countries then withheld **prorated** sums from their assessments, refusing to pay the portion of their assessment that would go to bond service. The end of the 1960s had established two unwritten rules: First, countries could withhold all or part of their assessed payments because of policy disputes. And second, countries could reduce their regular budget payments through targeted "withholdings."

To ease the financial strain, the General Assembly approved a plan to delay payment to countries supplying troops and equipment to peacekeeping operations. This meant that the United Nations essentially

A UN peacekeeper with a child in the Congo; the UN mission to the Congo in the 1960s was one of its most expensive to date, setting off a financial crisis for the United Nations.

The U.S. Congress, housed in the U.S. Capitol (above), is responsible for financing the payment of U.S. dues to the United Nations, the largest of all UN member nations, through the annual budget proposals Congress passes.

forced a loan onto these countries, some of them smaller or poor nations. In 1965, members were invited to contribute to a special account that acted as a reserve fund, expanding on another small fund set up in 1945. These two funds provided the United Nations with a small financial cushion. However, this would still prove to be inadequate to meet the needs of the growing organization.

U.S. Dues Payments. During this period, the United States paid its dues and peacekeeping assessments. By the 1980s, though, feelings in Washington had changed about the fairness of UN assessments. In 1983, the United States began to deny funding to UN programs that supported the Palestine Liberation Organization or SWAPO, an independence movement in Namibia. U.S. arrears continued to climb as the decade progressed, jumping from $12 million in 1984 to $86 million in 1985, forcing the United Nations to cut spending by 10 percent and lay off many staff.

The U.S. military budget takes precedence in Congress, and support for
the United Nations is often not considered a priority.

ONGOING NEEDS

Although financing for UN programs is precarious, the work left to be done by the world's only international governing body has greatly increased. According to the World Bank, in 2011, 17 percent of the people in the developing world lived on roughly $1.25 a day, a 43 percent drop from 1990, while 2.2 billion people lived on less than $2. However, at the current rate of progress 1 billion will continue to live in extreme poverty within the next few years. Meanwhile, disease, economic instability, and armed conflict also threaten much of the world.

By the end of the first Gulf War in 1991, Washington's debts equaled $240 million, down from an all-time high a few years before. Meanwhile, other countries' debts had risen, especially as economic recession hit the emerging economies of Eastern Europe, forcing such large payers as Russia and Ukraine into massive debt. At the end of 2014, the United States was around $180 million in arrears, the result of past amounts it has yet to pay off. While this might seem a large amount, the United States now pays its current dues on a regular basis. For 2014, that amounted to roughly $620 million.

Alternative Sources of Funding

It seems inevitable that the United Nations will have to develop additional ways to generate revenue. Worldwide taxes on currency trade, carbon emissions, and arms trade could counter many crises while at the same time raise revenue.

Taxing Monetary Transactions. The foreign currency exchange market is the largest market in the world, with an estimated $1.9 trillion currency traded per day. This means that in less than one year, currency worth ten times the global gross domestic product is traded. Economists have examined the possibility of levying a tax on international monetary transactions as a means to generate revenue. A tax rate ranging from 0.005 to 0.25 percent could generate between $15 and $300 billion per year, which would go far to promote international peace and development.

Carbon Taxes. A large body of research promotes the economic and environmental wisdom of energy taxes. Arguments in favor of such a tax rest on the assumption that free markets are unable to incorporate all of the relevant social costs of economic activity, including damage to the climate from fossil fuel emissions, into the end price of goods. Thus, the goal of an energy tax is to correct this by enabling the price of goods and services to reflect full social and environmental costs. Carbon taxes make the greatest sense because they tax emissions directly. Coal creates the greatest amount of carbon emissions and would therefore be taxed in greater proportion than oil and natural gas, which have lower carbon concentrations. This is also felt to be a fair way to impose a global tax because the tax would be passed on to individuals according to wealth, in direct proportion to the amount they consume.

Internet Taxes. An e-mail or Internet tax, also known as a "bit tax," seeks to introduce a tax on the amount of data sent through the Internet. Because of the volume of data sent via e-mail, the tax could be very slight and still generate a tremendous amount of revenue. A person sending a hundred e-mails a day, for instance, each containing a ten-kilobyte document, would pay a tax of just one cent, according to one proposal. Proponents of such a tax hope to raise funds that would be spent to close the "digital divide" between rich and poor.

The UNDP Human Development Report 1999 researched such a tax. The UNDP estimated that globally in 1996, this type of tax would have yielded $70 billion. Since Internet users now frequently send data-rich photos and large documents, transfer rates are far higher than in 1996,

Pictured here is Stockholm, the capital of Sweden. In the 1990s, Sweden instituted carbon taxes to help move the country away from fossil-fuel energy production. According to many, a global carbon tax would not only reduce carbon emissions, but could generate funding for the UN and other important intergovernmental organizations.

while the number of Internet users has grown. For these reasons, a tax could be set at a rate well below the one the UNDP first proposed. Still, it could produce a large boost to the UN's operating budget while impacting most users very little. There has been opposition to the "bit tax," especially in the United States where Congress has balked at the measure.

* * *

Many reforms are being made, both by the United Nations itself and by member nations to help end the serious financial crisis the organization faces. The United Nations is working to make the most out of every dollar it spends and to disclose its financial records more fully, giving those countries that fund the body more confidence that their money is being well spent. As the United Nations looks to the future, it is clear that there is much work to be done to promote peace and justice in the world.

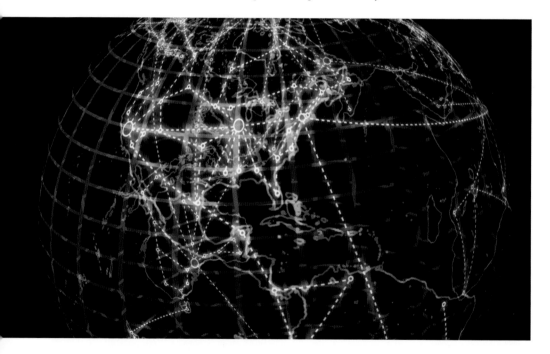

Internet communications span the globe, which means an e-mail tax could yield considerable financing for the United Nations.

CHAPTER SIX

TEXT-DEPENDENT QUESTIONS

1. How many people in developing countries live on less than $2 a day?

2. How much money did the United States owe the UN at the end of 2014?

3. Explain the concept of the "bit tax."

RESEARCH PROJECTS

1. Research the procedures of the General Assembly, and create a mock session of the General Assembly to discuss levying an e-mail tax to increase revenue. Have each student represent a different country and present their view of the tax. Which countries would likely support such a measure? Which countries would be against it?

2. Research the budget of the United Nations from its founding to the present, and then create a line chart.

TIME LINE

1815	The Holy Alliance is formed.
1825	The Holy Alliance is dissolved.
1864	The First Geneva Convention is adopted.
1914	World War I begins.
1919	Paris Peace Conference accepts Wilson's proposal to create the League of Nations. Treaty of Versailles signed.
1920	The first meeting of the League of Nations is held.
1926	Germany is admitted to the League of Nations.
1932	Japan withdraws from the League of Nations.
1933	Germany withdraws from the League of Nations.
1934	The Soviet Union joins the League of Nations.
1939	The Soviet Union is expelled from the League of Nations. World War II begins.
1945	World War II ends. The United Nations is founded.
1946	League of Nations dissolves itself, and all services, mandates, and property is transferred to the newly formed United Nations.

1963	Articles 23, 27, and 61 of the UN Charter are amended.
1965	Amendments to Articles 23, 27, and 61 take force.
1969	Amendment to Article 109 takes force.
1971	People's Republic of China replaces the Republic of China as China's representative to the United Nations.
1973	Second amendment to Article 61 takes force.
1991	Russia replaces the Soviet Union at the United Nations and on the Security Council.
2005	Special session of the General Assembly is held to commemorate the UN's sixtieth anniversary.
2006	The United Nations continues to seek new ways to fund its programs.
2011	Creation of the program called UN Women, which works for the elimination of discrimination of girls and women.
2014	Special Session of the General Assembly to follow up on the International Conference on Population and Development.

FURTHER RESEARCH

Books

Ginneken, Anique H. M. *The A to Z of the League of Nations*. Lanham, MD: Scarecrow Press, 2009.

Grant, R. G. *World War I: The Definitive Visual History*. New York: DK Publishing, 2014.

Holmes, Richard. *World War II: The Definitive Visual History*. New York: DK Publishing, 2009.

Pubantz, Jerry, and John Allphin Moore Jr. *Encyclopedia of the United Nations,* 2nd ed. New York: Facts On File, 2009.

Online Sources

Charter of the United Nations: www.un.org/en/documents/charter/

Office of the President of the General Assembly of the United Nations www.un.org/en/ga/

United States Mission to the United Nations www.usunnewyork.usmission.gov/

UN Secretary-General's Office: www.un.org/sg/

NOTE TO EDUCATORS: This book contains both imperial and metric measurements as well as references to global practices and trends in an effort to encourage the student to gain a worldly perspective. We, as publishers, feel it's our role to give young adults the tools they need to thrive in a global society.

SERIES GLOSSARY

abstain: not to vote for or against proposal when a vote is held.

Allies: the countries that fought against Germany in World War I or against the Axis powers in World War II.

ambassador: an official representative of one country to another country.

amendments: process of changing a legal document.

appeal: a formal request to a higher authority requesting a change of a decision.

appeasement: a deliberate attempt pacify a potentially troublesome nation.

arbitration: the process of resolving disputes through an impartial third party.

asylum: protection granted by a nation to someone who has left fled their country as a political refugee.

Axis: the alliance of Germany, Italy, and Japan that fought the allies in World War II.

blocs: groups of countries or political parties with the same goal.

bureaucracy: a complex system of administration, usually of a government or corporation.

capital: material wealth in the form of money or property.

civil law: law of a state dealing with the rights of private citizens.

coalition: in military terms, a group of nations joined together for a common purpose against a common enemy.

codification: the arrangement of laws into a systematic code.

Cold War: a largely nonviolent conflict between capitalist and communist countries following World War II.

compliance: conforming to a regulation or law.

conservation: preservation, management, and care of natural and cultural resources.

constitution: an official document outlining the rules of a system or government.

conventions: agreements between countries, less formal than treaties.

decolonization: the act of granting a colony its independence.

delegates: individuals chosen to represent or act on behalf of an organization or government.

demographic: characteristics of a human population.

diplomatic: having to do with international negotiations without resorting to violence.

disarmament: the reduction of a nation's supply of weapons or strength of its armed forces.

due process: the official procedures in legal cases required by law to ensure that the rights of all people involves are protected.

embargo: a government order limiting or prohibiting trade.

envoys: diplomats who act on behalf of a national government.

epidemic: a widespread occurrence of an infectious disease.

ethnic cleansing: the killing or imprisonment of an ethnic minority by a dominant group.

exchange rates: rates at which money of one country is exchanged the money of another.

extradition: the handing over by one government of someone accused of a crime in a different country for trial or punishment.

extremist: having to do with radical political or religious beliefs.

factions: smaller groups within larger groups that have opposing ideas.

fascist: relating to a system of government characterized by dictatorship, repression of opposition, and extreme nationalism.

flashpoints: areas of intense conflict and insecurity that often erupt into violent confrontation.

forgery: the act of making or producing an illegal copy of something.

free-market economy: economic system in which businesses operate without government control in matters such as pricing and wage levels.

genocide: systematic killing of all people from a national, ethnic, or religious group, or an attempt to do so.

globalization: the various processes that increase connections peoples of the world.

gross domestic product: total value of all goods and services produced within a country.

guerrilla: unorganized and small-scale warfare carried out by independent units.

human trafficking: the practice of seizing people against their will for the purpose of "selling" them for work, usually in the sex trade.

humanitarian: being concerned with or wanting to promote the well-being of other humans.

ideological: based on a specific system of beliefs, values, and ideas forming the basis of a social, economic, or political philosophy

indigenous: relating to the original inhabitants of an area or environment.

infrastructure: physical structures of a region, made up of roads, bridges, and so forth.

isolationism: the belief that a country should limit their involvement in the affairs of other countries.

mandate: an official instruction by an authority.

mediation: the process of resolving a dispute.

money laundering: the transferring of illegally obtained money through various businesses and accounts so as to hide it.

nationalists: people with an extreme sense of loyalty to their country.

nationalize: takeover by a government of a private business.

pandemic: a widespread epidemic in which a disease spreads to many countries and regions of the world.

per capita income: average amount earned by each individual in a country.

preamble: introduction, or opening words of a document.

precedent: established practice; a decision used as the basis of future decisions.

proliferation: the rapid spread of something.

propaganda: information or publicity put out by an organization or government to spread and promote a policy or idea.

protocols: preliminary memoranda often formulated and signed by diplomatic negotiators.

rapporteur: an official in charge of investigating and reporting to an agency, institution, or other entity.

ratification: the act of formally approving something.

referendum: a vote of the entire electorate on a question or questions put before it by the government or similar body.

reparation: compensation made by a nation defeated by others in a war.

sanction: a punishment imposed as a result of breaking a rule or law.

signatories: persons or governments who have signed a treaty and are bound by it.

sovereignty: self-rule, usually of a nation.

standard of living: the minimum amount of necessities essential to maintaining a comfortable life.

summit: a meeting between heads of government or other high-ranking officials.

sustainable: able to be maintained so that the resource is not depleted or damaged.

veto: the power of a person, country, or branch of government to reject the legislation of another.

INDEX

PICTURE CREDITS

BIOGRAPHIES

Author

HEATHER DOCALAVICH first became interested in the work of the United Nations while working as an adviser for a high school Model UN program. She lives in Hilton Head Island, South Carolina, with her four children.

Series Advisor

BRUCE RUSSETT is Dean Acheson Professor of Political Science at Yale University and editor of the Journal of Conflict Resolution. He has taught or researched at Columbia, Harvard, M.I.T., Michigan, and North Carolina in the United States, and educational institutions in Belgium, Britain, Israel, Japan, and the Netherlands. He has been president of the International Studies Association and the Peace Science Society, and holds an honorary doctorate from Uppsala University in Sweden. He was principal adviser to the U.S. Catholic Bishops for their pastoral letter on nuclear deterrence in 1985, and codirected the staff for the 1995 Ford Foundation report, *The United Nations in Its Second Half Century*. He has served as editor of the *Journal of Conflict Resolution* since 1973. The twenty-five books he has published include *The Once and Future Security Council* (1997), *Triangulating Peace: Democracy, Interdependence, and International Organizations* (2001), *World Politics: The Menu for Choice* (8th edition 2006), and *Purpose and Policy in the Global Community* (2006).